ABSOLUTE BEGINNERS
Piano

T0080137

Audio recorded, mixed and mastered by John Rose and Jonas Persson.
Music processed by Paul Ewers.
Backing tracks by Guy Dagul and Ed Lozano.
Edited by Heather Slater.

ISBN 978-0-8256-3528-1

World headquarters, contact:
Hal Leonard
7777 West Bluemound Road
Milwaukee, WI 53213
Email: info@halleonard.com

In Europe, contact:
Hal Leonard Europe Limited
42 Wigmore Street
Marylebone, London, W1U 2RY
Email: info@halleonardeurope.com

In Australia, contact:
Hal Leonard Australia Pty. Ltd.
4 Lentara Court
Cheltenham, Victoria, 3192 Australia
Email: info@halleonard.com.au

Contents

Introduction

Welcome to *Absolute Beginners Piano*.

This book will teach you all of the essential basics you need to know to play the piano, and will get you started playing—fast!

You'll start by playing short examples, and very soon you'll be playing whole pieces with both hands together.

The **easy-to-follow instructions** will guide you through:

- correct posture and playing position
- finding the notes on the piano keyboard
- reading basic music notation, learning note names, and understanding rhythm
- playing with hands separately and together

Listen to the audio as you learn—the audio will let you hear how the music should sound—and then try to play the piano part with the backing tracks.

And always remember: practice makes perfect! It's best to practice a small amount often because you are teaching your muscles to memorize certain repeated actions. Twenty minutes each day is far better than two hours on the weekend with nothing in between.

No matter what type of music you want to play— classical, jazz, popular—the basic techniques are all the same. Once you master them, you'll be well on your way to playing in whatever style you prefer.

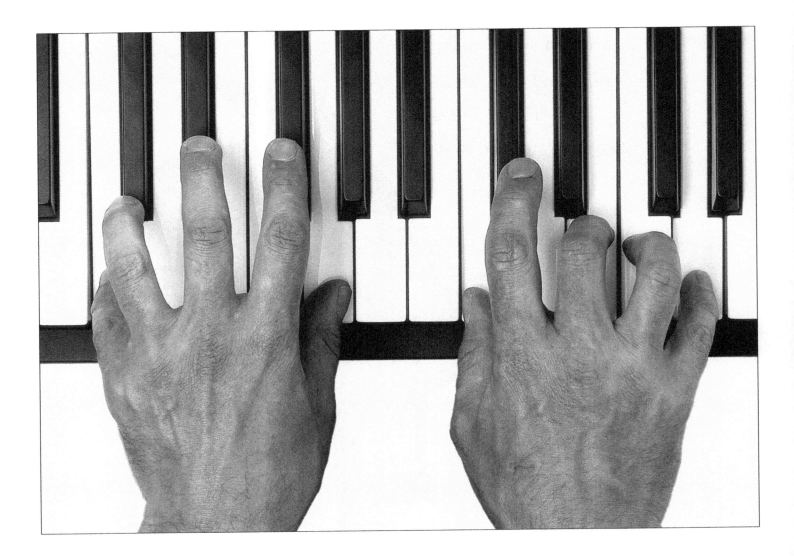

A good **playing position** means that you'll be comfortable at the piano, and this will help you to play well.

Sit facing the middle of the piano keyboard with your feet directly in front of the pedals, and try to keep your back reasonably straight. Avoid tension in any part of your body, particularly in your lower arms.

If you sit too high or too low, you'll find it more difficult to play accurately—and your arms will get tired very quickly!

Also make sure you are sitting a comfortable distance away from the keyboard. If you sit too far away you'll find it hard to reach the upper and lower notes, and if you sit too close you'll be restricting your arm movement.

You will find it easier to play if you keep your fingernails quite short so that the pads of your fingers, and not your fingernails, are making direct contact with the keys.

When playing the piano, wear something comfortable so that your arms can move freely.

Ideally your seat should be at a height which allows your forearms to sit level with, or just above, the piano keyboard. An adjustable piano stool is preferable to an ordinary chair because it will allow for adjustments according to your height.

Make sure that you keep your wrists up and steady, and don't let your wrists drop to or below the level of the keyboard.

Correct

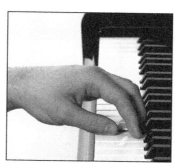

Incorrect

Fingering

Fingering is a system that assigns certain fingers to certain notes on the piano keyboard, and it's what keeps your fingers from getting tangled up in knots when you play!

This is how it works: each finger on each hand is given a number from 1 to 5, as shown in the photograph below. You will see these numbers over the notes in the music—they tell you which finger to use when you are playing a particular note.

Try to stick to the recommended fingerings for each piece and you'll soon get into the habit of having your hands in the correct position.

Left hand

Right hand

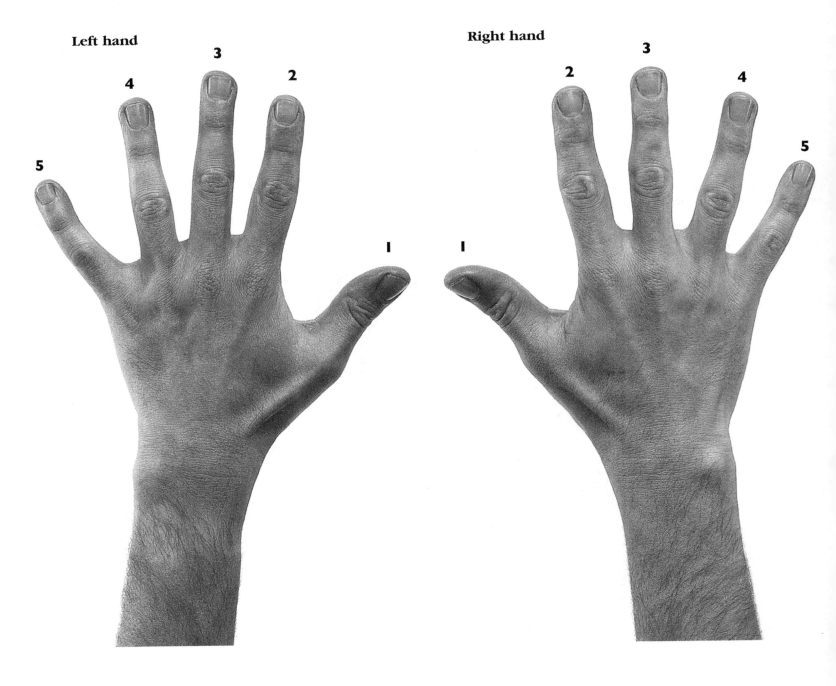

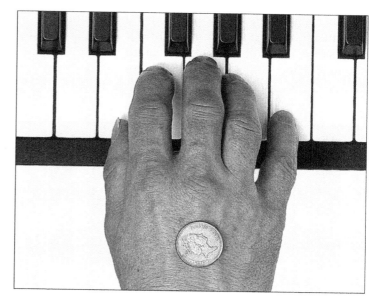

Tip

Try resting a small coin on the back of your hand as you place your hands on the piano keyboard. You should be able to play quite comfortably without the coin falling off!

Proper **hand position** involves both your fingers and your wrists. Your hand should be supported from the wrist, and it's very important that you don't let your wrist fall below keyboard level.

With your fingers sitting lightly above the keys, curl them slightly as if you're holding an imaginary ball.

Or try this: Place your relaxed hand on your knee so that it is covering your kneecap. Then, carefully lift your hand from your knee to the keyboard and it will be in the proper, curved position.

Your fingertips should cover five adjacent notes in each hand, as in the photo below. This is the normal five-finger position, and this is how you should begin when you are playing the exercises in this book.

Finding Your Way Around

At first glance, the piano keyboard may seem confusing—there are so many notes! But it is actually the same series of 12 notes repeated over and over again for the entire length of the keyboard. Only 7 letter names are used: C, D, E, F, G, A, and B.

The black keys are arranged in twos and threes in a repeating pattern. This pattern is very useful because it helps you to find your way around the keyboard.

These are the notes you will learn in this book:

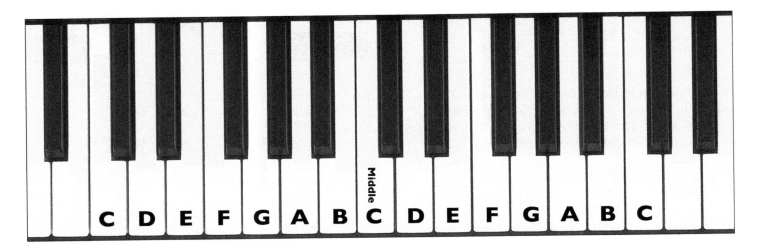

C D E F G A B C(Middle) D E F G A B C

How the piano works

The word "piano" is short for "pianoforte," which is an Italian term meaning "soft-loud."

The piano was given this name because the volume of its sound is controlled by the force with which the keys are struck—in other words, a piano, unlike an electronic keyboard, can be played quietly or loudly, or at any volume in between.

There are many types of pianos, but they are all constructed in basically the same way. The inside of a piano looks a bit like a harp, with strings ranging in size from quite thick for the low notes, to very thin for the high notes.

The sound is produced when these strings are struck by small felt-covered "hammers," which spring into action when you strike a key.

Reading music

Reading music is really quite easy once you understand the fundamentals.

A musical note has just two properties: **pitch** and **duration**. Pitch tells you how high or low a note is—low is to the left on the keyboard, and high is to the right—and duration tells you how long the note should last and when it is to be played in relation to the other notes.

The five lines on which the notes are placed are called a **staff**. A note placed on the top of the staff will sound higher than a note placed on the bottom.

For piano players there is one staff for the right hand and one for the left hand. For the first part of this book we'll be using only the right hand.

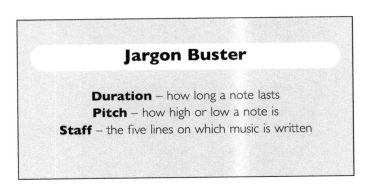

Jargon Buster

Duration – how long a note lasts
Pitch – how high or low a note is
Staff – the five lines on which music is written

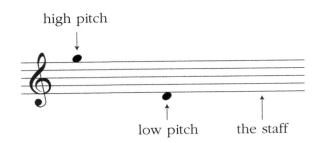

high pitch

low pitch   the staff

The same five lines (the staff) that we use for music played by the right hand are also used for music played by the left hand. To indicate which notes are to be played by which hand, we use a **clef**.

For the right hand we use a **treble clef**:

For the left hand we use a **bass clef**:

You'll notice that these clefs are each anchored on the staff at a specific point, and this can help you to identify the notes.

The treble clef curls around the second line of the staff (from bottom to top), which is the note G:

The bass clef is anchored around the note F:

In the example above, notice that the two dots to the right of the bass clef are at either side of the line upon which the note F sits.

Using these clues—the treble clef curls around G and the bass clef's dots surround F—you can work out the position of every note on the staff, for both the right and left hand.

Jargon Buster

A **clef** (French for "key") is the symbol that appears at the beginning of every piece of music. The **treble clef** is used for right-hand notes, the **bass clef** is used for left-hand notes.

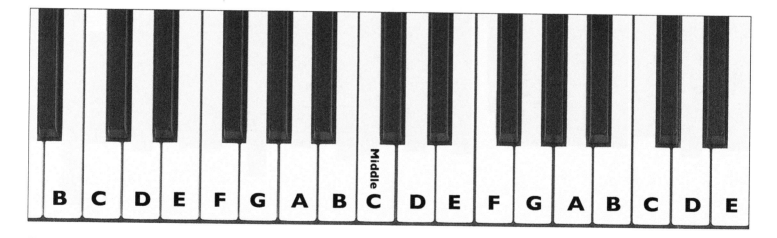

CHECKPOINT

WHAT YOU'VE LEARNED SO FAR...

You can now:

- Position your hands and wrists on the keyboard correctly
- Find your way around the piano keyboard
- Understand basic concepts of pitch and rhythm

Rhythm

Music has a basic **rhythm**, or **pulse**. When you tap your foot to a song, you are responding to the rhythm of the music.

Rhythm is created when multiples of **beats** are grouped together into larger units called **bars**, or **measures**. This pattern of beats determines the rhythm of a piece of music.

To get used to counting "in time," try the following exercise. Count steadily from 1 to 4 and then repeat the sequence a few times, like this:

1 - 2 - 3 - 4 / 1 - 2 - 3 - 4 / 1 - 2 - 3 - 4 / repeat...

Each time you count "1" you are at the beginning of a new bar. It's that simple!

Note values

If you look at a piece of music you'll see that notes have different shapes—some have tails, some have solid noteheads, while others are hollow. Each type of note lasts for a different number of beats.

Time signatures

At the beginning of every piece of music, you will see a **time signature**. The most common time signature is 4/4, which looks like this:

A time signature tells you how many notes of what value to play in each bar. The bottom number represents the note value, and the top number represents the number of those notes that will fit into each bar. So in **4/4 time**, there are 4 quarter notes per bar.

Tip

4/4 time is sometimes called **common time**, represented with a time signature that looks like this:

C

A note that looks like this **o** is called a **whole note**. A whole note lasts for the duration of a full bar—in other words, it has a count of four beats. You would count a whole note like this:

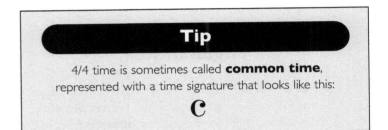

This note ♩ is called a **half note**, and it lasts for two beats. A half note is counted like this:

This note ♩ is called a **quarter note**, and it lasts for one beat. There are four quarter notes to every bar and they are counted like this:

You can put any combination of these notes in a bar as long as they add up to four. So, as you can see, rhythm is quite a bit like basic math! You now know enough about rhythm to play some music.

Let's find your first note: **Middle C**.

Middle C is a white key, and the easiest way to locate a white key is to see where it fits into the pattern of black keys.

Look for the groups of two black keys, and then find the note right in the middle—you have just found the note D. C is directly to the left of D, or to the left of the group of two black keys.

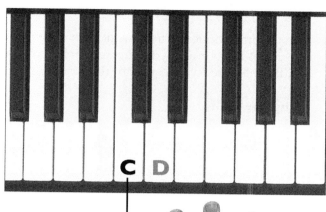

You'll notice that the groups of black keys are repeated all the way up the piano keyboard, so there are many different Cs. In order to distinguish between them we usually refer to one of them as Middle C, which is, just as you would expect, the one closest to the center of the piano keyboard.

Locate Middle C on your piano—on most pianos, it is the closest C to the manufacturer's label.

Now try to play a few different Cs. The diagram below shows you how to find the C below Middle C and the C above Middle C.

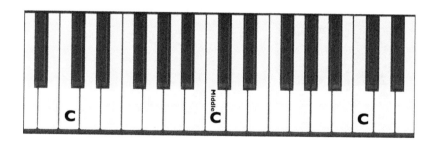

Jargon Buster

A **ledger line** is a tiny horizontal line placed just above or below the staff, which allows us to write notes which are higher or lower than the staff. Middle C is an example of a note that is written on a ledger line.

This is what Middle C looks like on the staff:

Notice that Middle C is written on a small line directly under the main staff. This is called a **ledger line**, and it allows us to write notes that are higher or lower than the staff's five lines and four spaces. It is important that you can tell one C from another, or else you might play the right notes (according to their name) but in the wrong place on the keyboard!

The examples on the next few pages all use Middle C and the notes just above it.

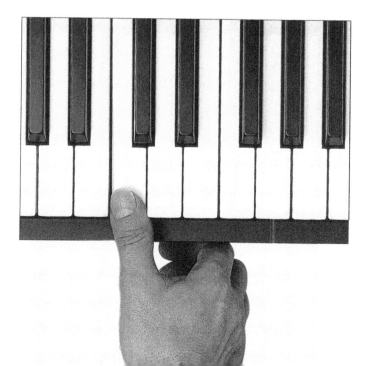

Your First Exercise

Now you're ready to play your first piece.

Don't worry about reading music—as long as you can count to four and you can remember where Middle C is, then you can play this piece!

Using the audio

The audio included with this book will help you. On Track 1, you will hear a demonstration of the piece below played with a backing track.

On Track 2, you will hear just the backing track so you can try it yourself.

After the four-beat intro click, play a Middle C for four beats with the accompanying music, then rest for four beats, then play for four and rest for four, and so on until the end of the piece.

The symbol ▬ is called a rest, and it is there to tell you when not to play. You'll learn more about rests a bit further on in this book.

The piece lasts for eight bars. This means that you'll be counting to four 8 times in a row. This may seem simple, but already you're teaching yourself the important discipline of playing in time.

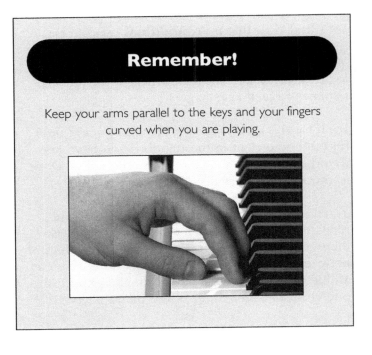

Remember!

Keep your arms parallel to the keys and your fingers curved when you are playing.

Learning to count regular beats is something that you will eventually do automatically. But for now, it will help to count out loud while you are playing.

Track 1 on the recording demonstrates how this piece should sound, and **Track 2** gives you a backing track that you can play along with.

Count: 1 2 3 4   1 2 3 4   1 2 3 4   1 2 3 4   etc.

Now you're ready to learn two more notes—but first, take a moment to review the pattern of keys on the keyboard, as shown below:

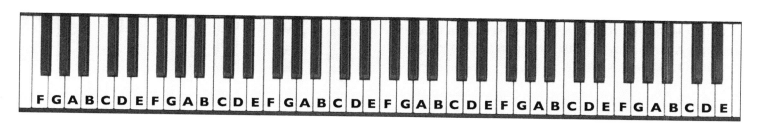

Here is the note D, which you first found in between the groups of 2 black notes. Make sure you are playing the D directly to the right of Middle C.

D

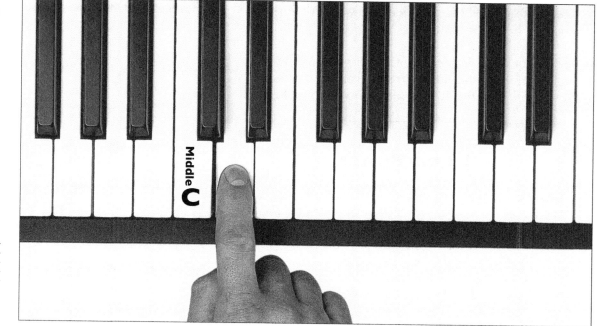

Just to the right of D is the note E:

E

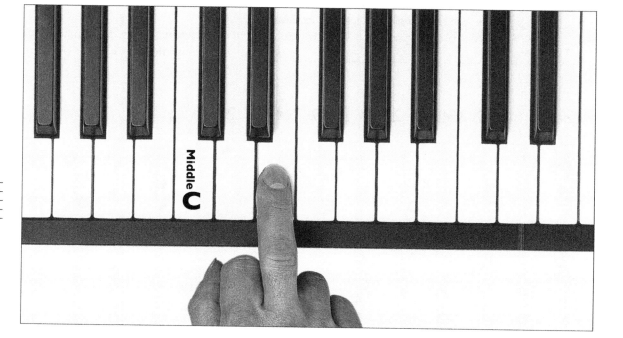

Now you know three notes—play every group of C-D-E that you can find on the keyboard, naming them out loud as you go.

Below is a tune that will help you remember these notes. Always play C with the thumb of your right hand (1), D with your index finger (2), and E with your middle finger (3). Say the names of the notes as you play them, and allow four beats (or one bar) per note.

Watch out for the one bar of rest after each group of three notes. The beat numbers are written over the music to help you count.

Keep your hand in a relaxed position, avoiding tension in your shoulders, lower arms, and hands. Press each note firmly and play smoothly, or **legato**.

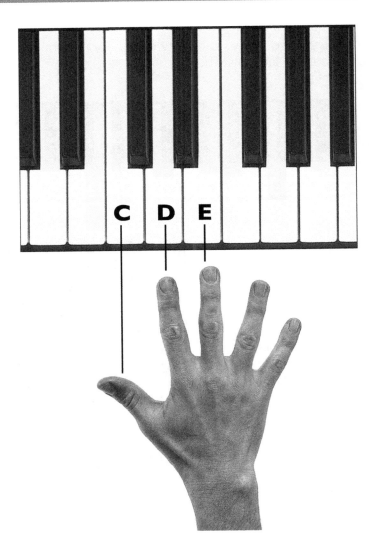

Jargon Buster

Legato (Italian for "smoothly") is a term used to describe the way in which successive notes are played on the piano. To play legato, hold each note just until you have played the next one and release the first note at the exact moment you strike the second one. This will ensure that one note does not overlap with the next, and that there are no "gaps" between notes.

The opposite of legato is **staccato** ("detached"), which means that the notes are not joined together, but are shortened instead so that there are gaps between notes. In this book, you will only be playing legato, so be aware of this concept of playing smoothly, with no gaps.

Keep the tempo slow to start, gradually increasing speed as you become more confident.

Listen to the demonstration on **Track 3** and then play along with the backing track on **Track 4**.

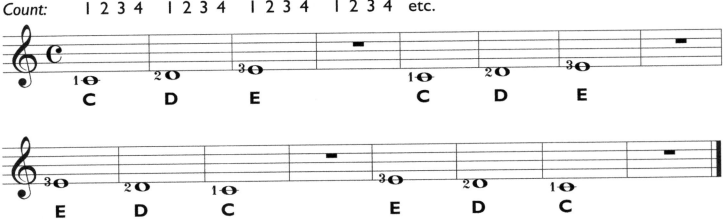

Now practice the notes C, D, and E with the following exercises before going on to play your first complete song, "Merrily We Roll Along."

Before you play any exercise or song, always remember to first take a look at the time signature, starting hand position, and suggested fingerings.

Exercise #1

Exercise #2

Exercise #3

Track 5 Demonstration
Track 6 Backing track

Merrily We Roll Along *Traditional*

New Notes F, G, A, and B

F

G

A

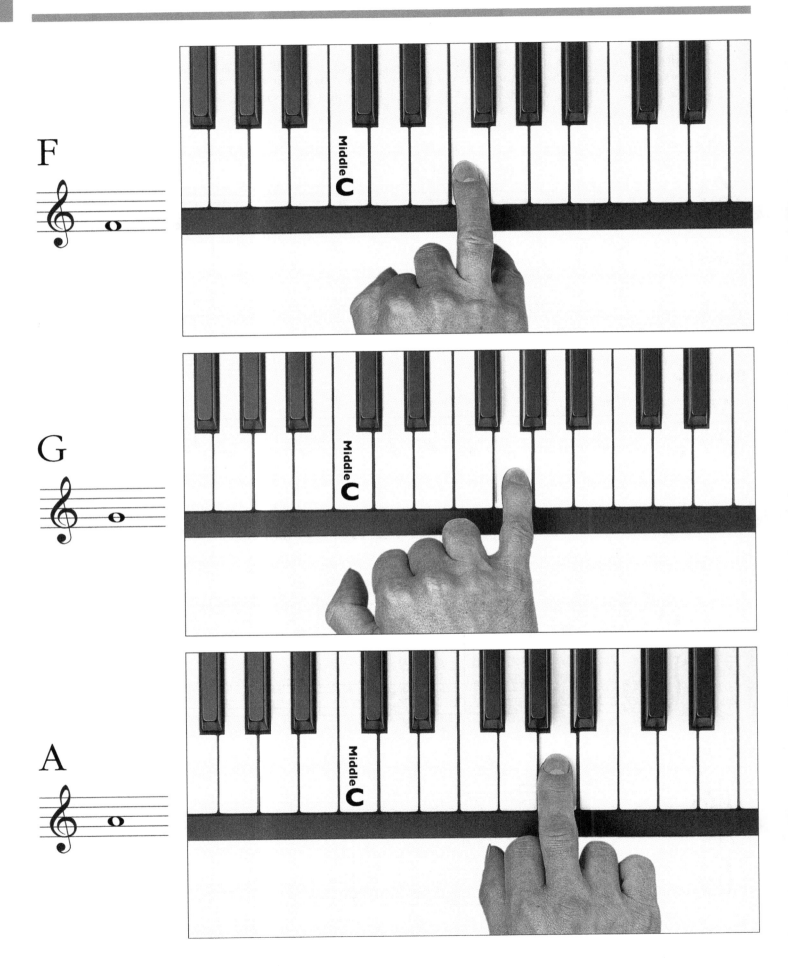

Remember, you can use the pattern of the black notes to help you find the white ones. Look at the diagram below, and notice the repeating pattern of three black keys.

Reading from left to right, the notes you've just learned are **F, G, A,** and **B**. Practice finding each note and say the letter names out loud as you play.

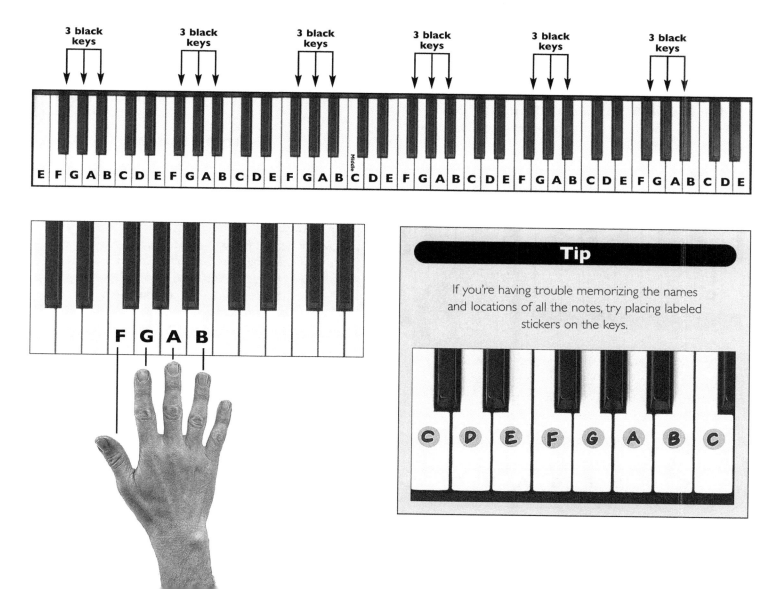

Tip

If you're having trouble memorizing the names and locations of all the notes, try placing labeled stickers on the keys.

Playing F to B and a New C

Now that you know how to count beats and bars, let's try an exercise that will familiarize you with your new notes.

This exercise will also let you count in a new way, as each note has two beats instead of one—in other words, you will be playing **half notes** instead of quarter notes.

For this exercise play the lower note (F) with the thumb of your right hand. Keep the relaxed hand position you learned earlier, with your other fingers "hovering" over the other notes.

Listen to the demonstration on **Track 7** and then play along with the backing track on **Track 8**.

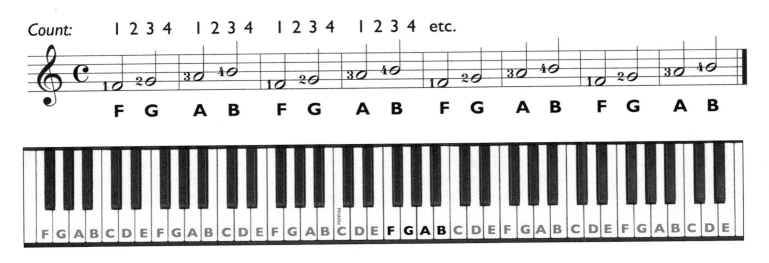

Count: 1 2 3 4   1 2 3 4   1 2 3 4   1 2 3 4   etc.

A new note in the right hand

So far, you have learned to play seven notes, from Middle C up to B. The note to the right of B is another C—this note is one **octave**, or eight notes, higher than Middle C.

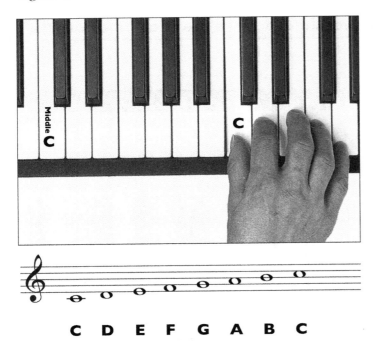

C D E F G A B C

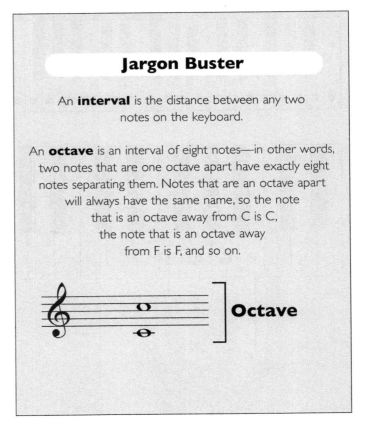

Jargon Buster

An **interval** is the distance between any two notes on the keyboard.

An **octave** is an interval of eight notes—in other words, two notes that are one octave apart have exactly eight notes separating them. Notes that are an octave apart will always have the same name, so the note that is an octave away from C is C, the note that is an octave away from F is F, and so on.

Octave

Now you can play the popular tune "Lightly Row" using the notes Middle C to G that you learned in the right hand. Remember to keep your fingers hovering over the keys so that you are always in a proper playing position and ready for the next note.

Listen to the demonstration on **Track 9** and then play along with the backing track on **Track 10**.

Lightly Row *Traditional*

Left-Hand C, D, and E

Here are your first notes in the bass clef, to be played with your left hand.

C

D

E

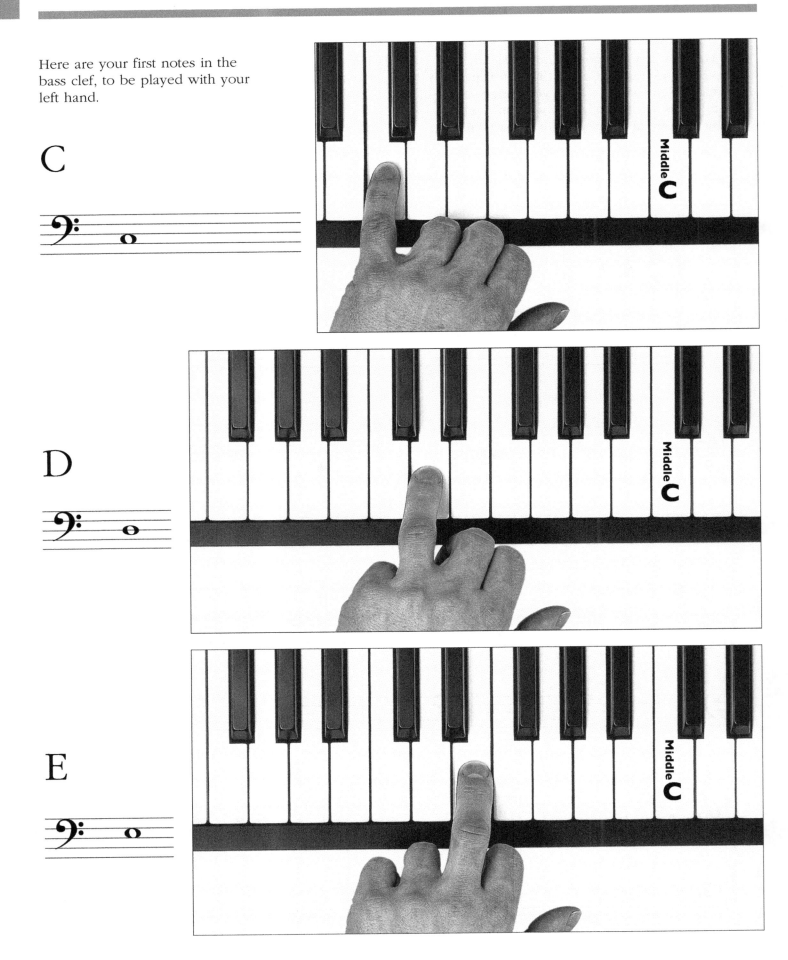

Now practice the notes C, D, and E in the left hand with the following exercises.

Once you have become comfortable with these notes in the left hand, go on to play your first left-hand song, "Au Clair De La Lune."

Exercise #1

Exercise #2

Exercise #3

Track 11 Demonstration
Track 12 Backing track

Au Clair De La Lune *Debussy*

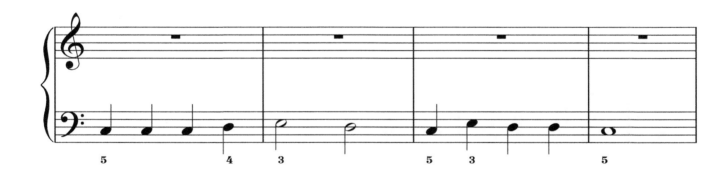

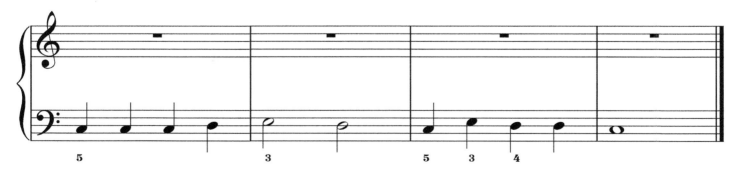

Left-Hand F and G

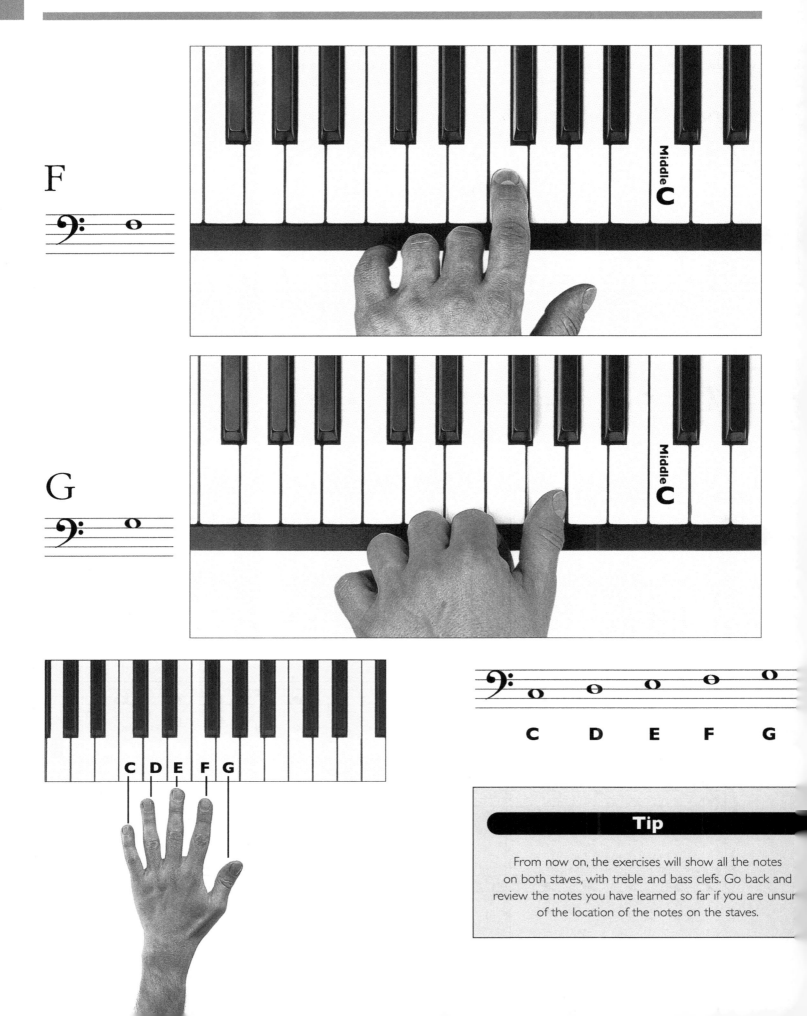

Tip

From now on, the exercises will show all the notes on both staves, with treble and bass clefs. Go back and review the notes you have learned so far if you are unsure of the location of the notes on the staves.

Track 13 Demonstration
Track 14 Backing track

Ode To Joy *Beethoven*

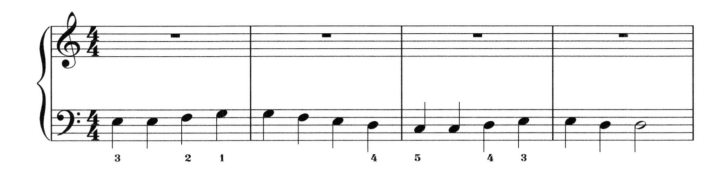

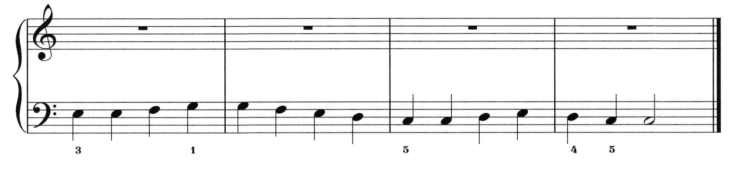

Track 15 Demonstration
Track 16 Backing track

Frère Jacques *Traditional*

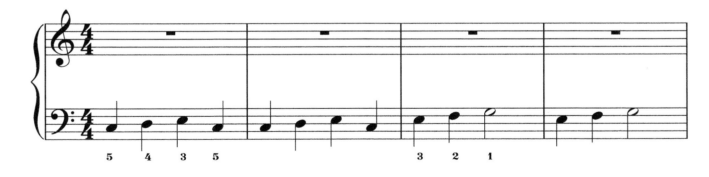

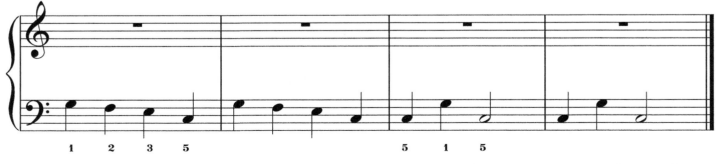

Playing Notes and Rests

This exercise is designed to get you used to playing with your left hand. It also introduces a new time signature: **cut time**. In cut time, quarter notes are counted as eighth notes—instead of receiving a full beat, they receive half a beat, and are counted as 1+2+ instead of 1-2-3-4 as in common time.

Count the rests even though you're not playing—that way you will always stay in time.

Listen to the demonstration on **Track 17** and then play along with the backing track on **Track 18**.

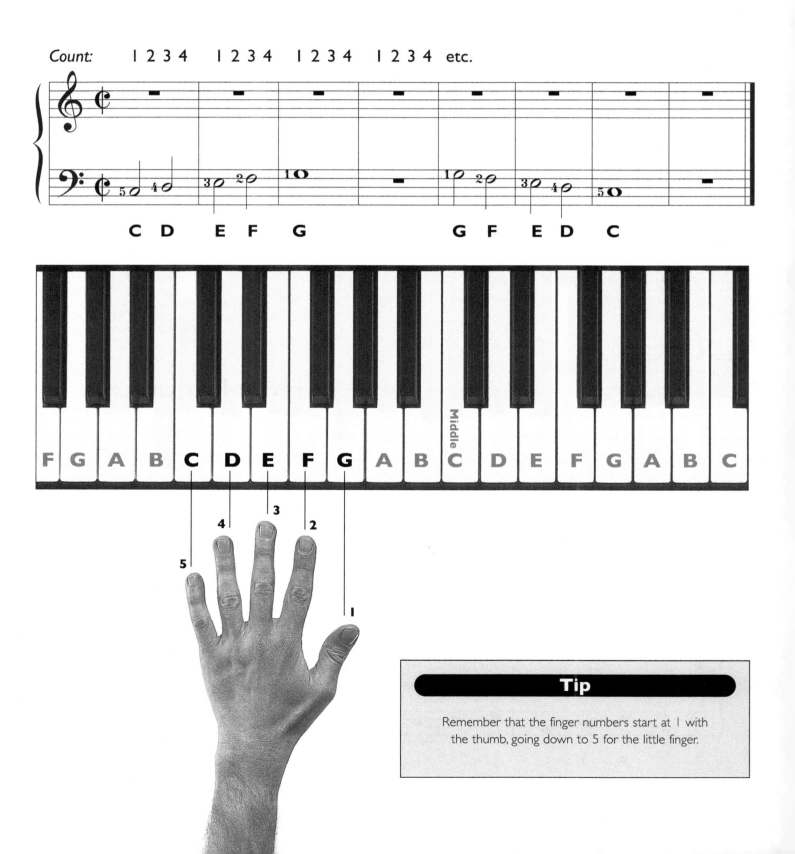

Tip

Remember that the finger numbers start at 1 with the thumb, going down to 5 for the little finger.

ABSOLUTE BEGINNERS
Piano Guide

The Piano Keyboard

There are only seven letter names used in music:

A-B-C-D-E-F-G

These seven letter names repeat over and
over again on the piano keyboard. The black keys
are arranged in groups of twos and threes.

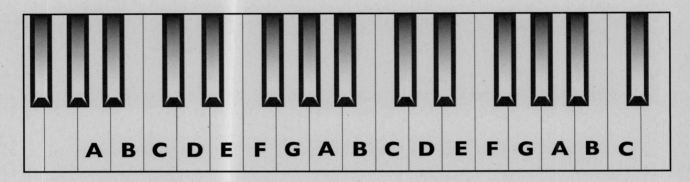

How to Learn the White Keys: C, D, and E

Use the black keys to locate the white keys.
For example, "D" lies between two black keys.

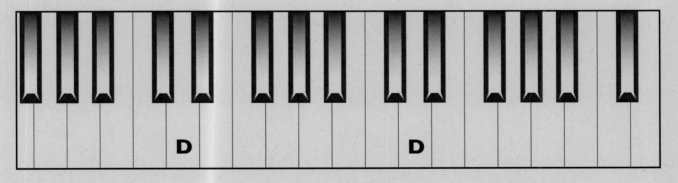

To the left of D lies C. To the right of D lies E.

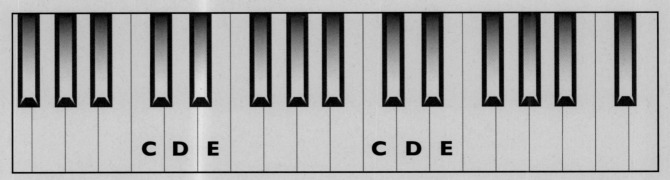

How to Learn the White Keys: F, G, A, and B

Use the groups of three black keys to locate F, G, A, and B
(the remaining four letters of the musical alphabet):

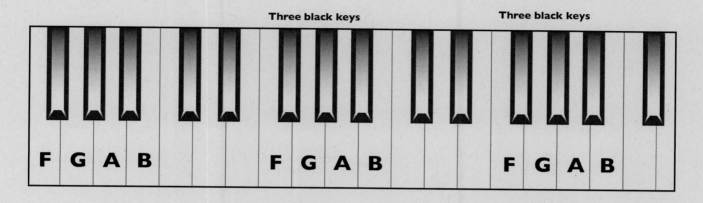

Find all the Fs, Gs, As, and Bs on your piano. Play each
note in turn and name it as you play.

You now know all the white notes and their names.

An Important Note: Middle C

One of the most important notes on the piano
is Middle C. This is the C nearest the middle of
the instrument, directly opposite the manufacturer's
name, as you sit at the piano.

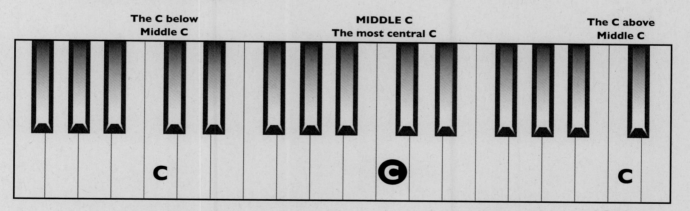

Look at the illustration above.

You will see three Cs:

- **The C below Middle C**
- **Middle C**
- **The C above Middle C**

Try to locate these Cs on your piano keyboard.

Here is an easy way to learn how to find them:

- Play Middle C with the right hand (any finger).
- Play Middle C with the left hand.
- Play the C below Middle C with the left hand.
- Play the C above Middle C with the right hand.
- Finally, play Middle C again with one of the
  fingers of each hand.

You now know how to find Middle C and
the Cs immediately above and below it.

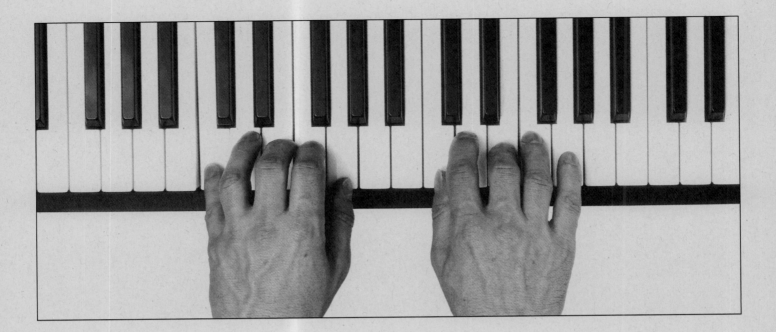

Sitting Correctly

It is important to sit correctly at the piano. The more comfortable you are, the easier it will be to play well.

Sit facing the middle of the instrument, with your feet right in front of the pedals. Sit upright, keeping your back as straight as possible but not rigid. Your seat should be high enough to allow your arms to be level with the keyboard, and you should sit far enough away that your arms have full range of movement.

Five-Finger Playing Position

With the tips of your fingers, cover five adjacent white notes in each hand. This is the normal five-finger playing position.

Always return to this position when you have been playing on other parts of the keyboard. Like a good tennis player always occupying the center of the court, this is the best "alert" position for piano players.

Hand Position

Support your hands from the wrists, which should be in a steady position. If you move your wrists too much as you play, you will soon experience muscle fatigue.

Curve your fingers as if you are gently holding an imaginary ball. Don't extend your fingers into the keys; instead, allow the natural position of your hand to determine which part of the key you depress with the tip of your finger.

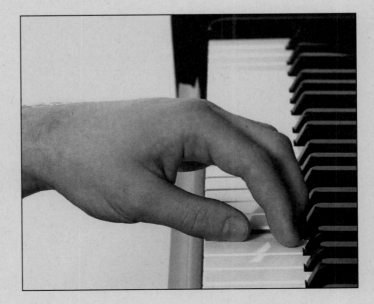

So far, most of the pieces you have played have been in stepwise motion—that is, the notes sit right beside each other on the keyboard. Now you will play a piece in which the notes are several steps apart. Bass lines often move this way, so it's important that you train your left hand to play these patterns.

If you concentrate on keeping your hand in the right position and follow the fingering numbers, you'll soon get it.

Listen to the demonstration on **Track 19** and then play along with the backing track on **Track 20**.

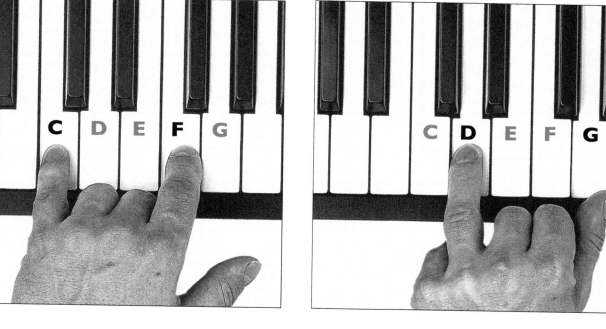

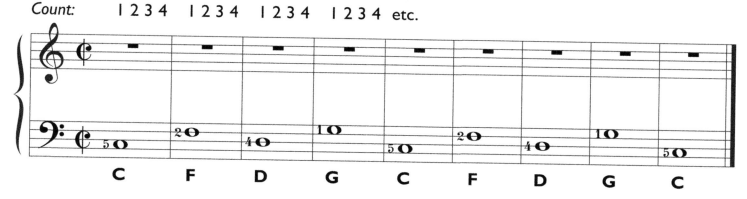

Intervals in the left hand

In this exercise, your left hand is moving over a distance, or **interval**, of four notes (from C to F, and then from D to G). An interval of four notes is called a **fourth** because there are four notes separating the top note from the bottom note.

Similarly, when the top and bottom notes are five notes apart, this interval is called a **fifth**. Bass lines often move in intervals of fourths and fifths.

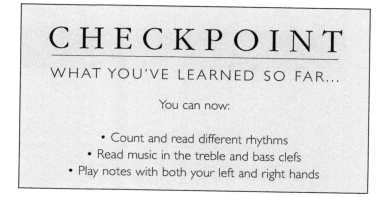

CHECKPOINT
WHAT YOU'VE LEARNED SO FAR...

You can now:

• Count and read different rhythms
• Read music in the treble and bass clefs
• Play notes with both your left and right hands

Hands Together, Ties, and Rests

Now you are ready to play with both hands at the same time.

Take a close look at the exercise at the top of the next page before you play. Notice that in the last bar of the piece, you only play for one beat—the remainder of the bar is filled with rests.

Also notice the curved lines joining the notes in the last bar to the notes in the second-last bar. They are called ties, and they simply add the value of one note to the other.

For example, if a whole note (4 beats) is tied to a half note (2 beats), you hold it for a total of 6 beats:

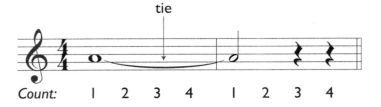

Count: 1   2   3   4   1   2   3   4

Look at the last two bars of the exercise on the next page. With your left hand, you'll play a C whole note in the second-last bar—then, instead of restriking the C in the last bar, you will hold the whole note you just played for one extra beat (as indicated by the tie, which leads to a quarter note).

So the last C in the left hand lasts for 5 beats (4+1), and the E in the right hand lasts for three beats (2+1).

Take your time with this exercise, and make sure you are confident with your counting and with the movement of your left hand before moving on.

Now that you are familiar with the note names, you'll no longer see them written directly below the music.

Listen to the demonstration on **Track 21** and then play along with the backing track on **Track 22**.

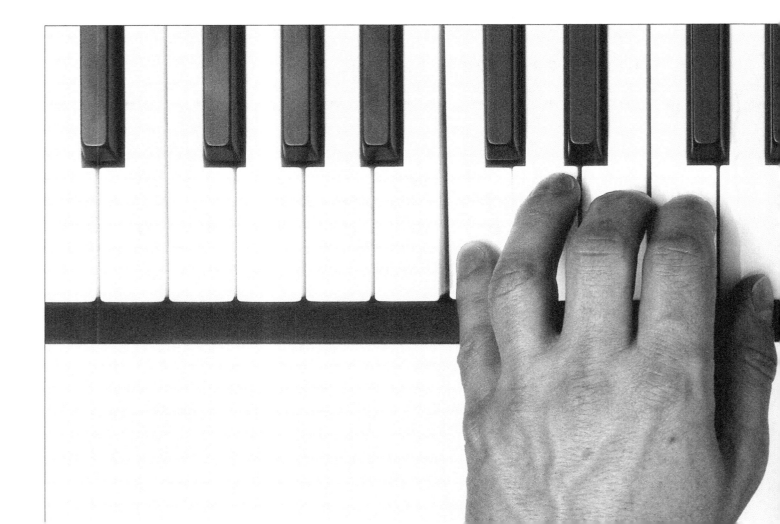

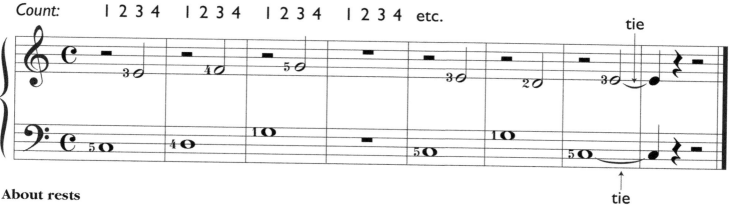

About rests

Rests tell us when not to play, and they have the same rhythmic values as their corresponding notes. You've already played pieces that contain rests, but let's take a closer look at the different types of rests.

A **whole-note rest** lasts for four beats, and looks like this:

A **half-note rest** lasts for two beats, and looks like this:

A **quarter-note rest** lasts for one beat, and looks like this:

Just like different notes, you can combine different rests. For example, for a silence of three beats, you could combine a half-note rest (2 beats) with a quarter-note rest (1 beat), like this:

New Notes and Review

Well done! You now know eight notes in the right hand and five notes in the left hand. Take a moment to review the notes you know.

To review, play through all of your notes very slowly, reminding yourself of the note name and its relation to the staff and the keyboard.

Right-hand review

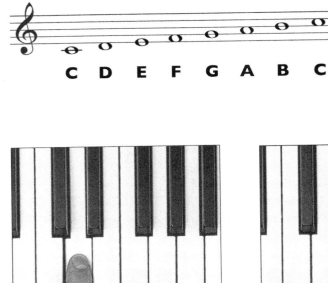

C D E F G A B C

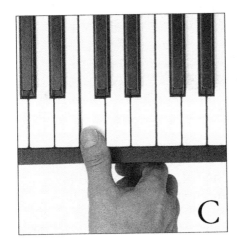

C

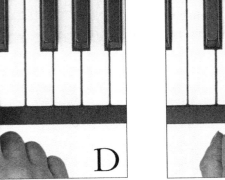

D

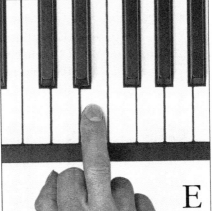

E

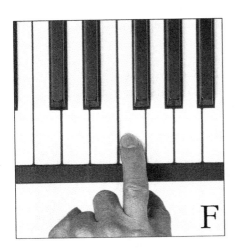

F

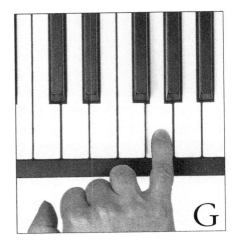

G

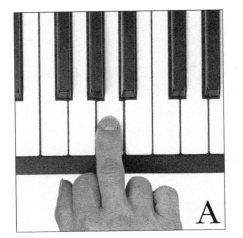

A

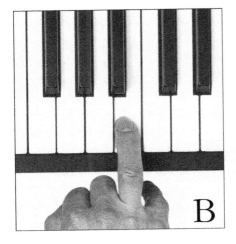

B

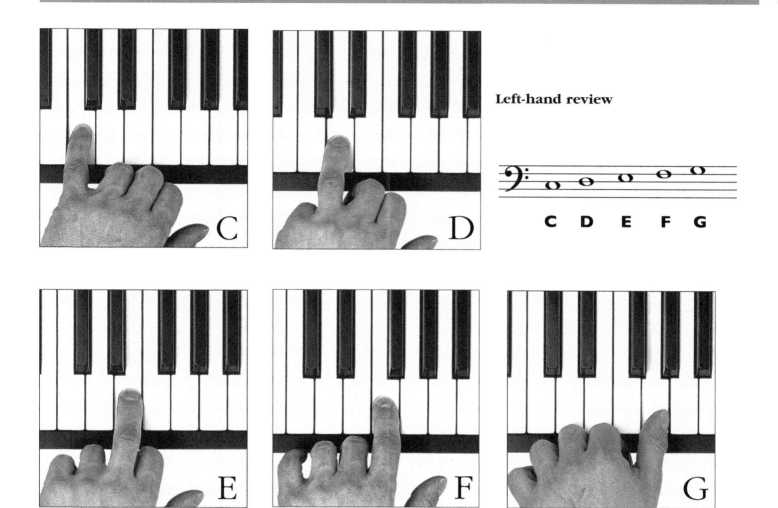

Left-hand review

C D E F G

Your last new notes!

To play the rest of the music in this book, you need to learn just a few more new notes: A, B, and C in the left hand, and A and B in the right hand.

These notes are usually played with the thumbs, as in the diagram below. Now you can play two octaves, from the C below middle C to the C above.

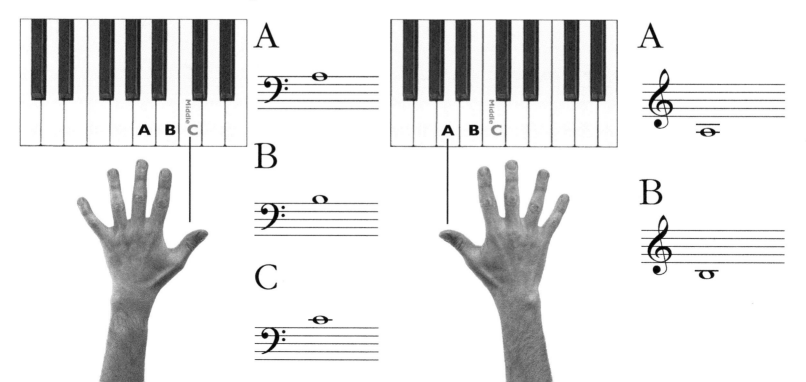

First Songs for Two Hands

Kum Ba Yah *Traditional*

Track 23 Demonstration
Track 24 Backing track

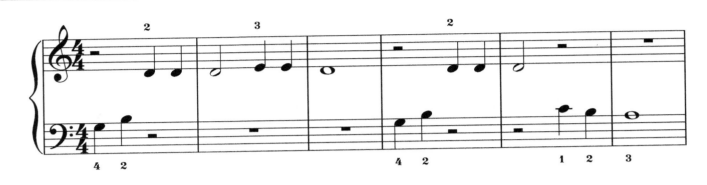

Track 25 Demonstration
Track 26 Backing track

Little Brown Jug *Traditional*

Listen to the demonstration on **Track 27** and then
play along with the backing track on **Track 28**.

Trumpet Voluntary *J. Clarke*

Eighth Notes and Repeat Signs

You've already played quarter notes, half notes, and whole notes. Now you'll learn about a new note value—the **eighth note**. An eighth note lasts for just one half of one beat. In other words, an eighth note is the equivalent of one half of a quarter note.

In a 4/4 bar, eighth notes are counted like this:

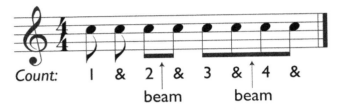

An easy way to remember the duration of a quarter note compared to an eighth note is to call a quarter note "tea" and two eighth notes "coffee." Look at the example below and say the words under the staff rhythmically:

	Tip
	When an eighth note is on its own, it is written with a curved flag attached to the stem. When there are two or more eighth notes in a row, they are bracketed together with a beam, which makes them easier to read.

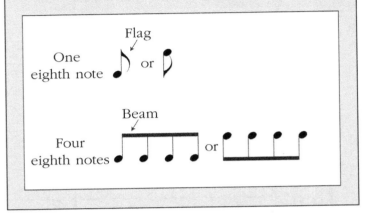

Here is a tune full of quarter notes and eighth notes.

Before you play, speak the words in time. Then play at a slow tempo and count with a steady beat so you can focus on accuracy. Practice it a few times slowly until you can speed up and still be accurate.

Notice the symbol :‖ at the end of the piece. This is called a **repeat sign**. This means that you need to go back to the beginning and play the whole piece one more time.

Listen to the demonstration on **Track 29** and then play along with the backing track on **Track 30**.

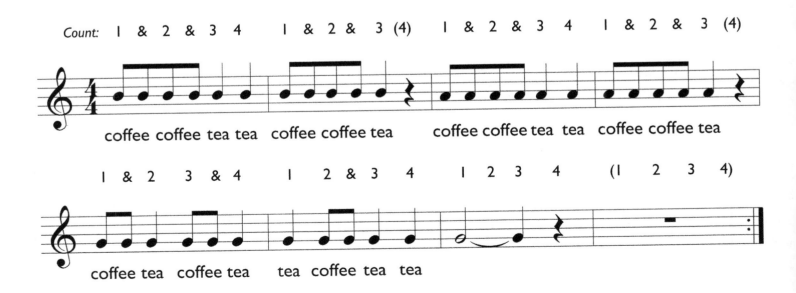

You will often see a small dot just to the right of a note. This dot is similar to a tie, in that it extends the duration of a note. A **dotted note** is held for an additional half of its original value—so a dotted quarter note would be held for a beat and a half. Clap this rhythm while counting out loud:

| & 2 & 3 & 4 &

Jargon Buster

The term **dotted note** refers to a note that has a small dot just to its right. This dot extends the duration of the note by one-half of its original value.

Now, keep counting but clap only the notes shown below:

1 (& 2) & 3 (& 4) & 1 (& 2) & 3 (& 4) & 1 (& 2) & 3 (& 4) & 1 (& 2) & 3 (& 4) &

Now play the example below, counting carefully so that the eighth notes fall in exactly the right place.

Listen to **Track 31** for a demonstration of the exercise below and play along for practice.

Here is an excerpt from Franz Schubert's Symphony No. 9, which has dotted notes in the right hand.

Listen to the demonstration on **Track 32** and then play along with the backing track on **Track 33**.

Waltz Rhythm (3/4)

The music you have played so far has been in 4/4 time—you have been playing 4 quarter-note beats per bar. Another common grouping of beats is 3/4, which means that there are 3 quarter-note beats per bar. This is sometimes called **"waltz rhythm"**—hum a few bars of a waltz and you'll know exactly what 3/4 time feels like!

Or, try this—count steadily to 3 and keep repeating. Emphasize the "1" each time you say it to get the feel of waltz rhythm:

1 - 2 - 3 / 1 - 2 - 3 / 1 - 2 - 3 etc.

When you are playing in 3/4 time you will often encounter this note ♩. This is a **dotted half note,** and it lasts for 3 beats.

You'll remember that a dot to the right of a note extends the note's duration by one-half—so a dotted half note is worth its original 2 beats plus 1 more (a quarter note) to equal 3:

The exercise below is in 3/4 time. Count a few bars in your head before starting to play, and practice slowly until you are confident with 3/4 time.

Listen to the demonstration on **Track 34** and then play along with the backing track on **Track 35**.

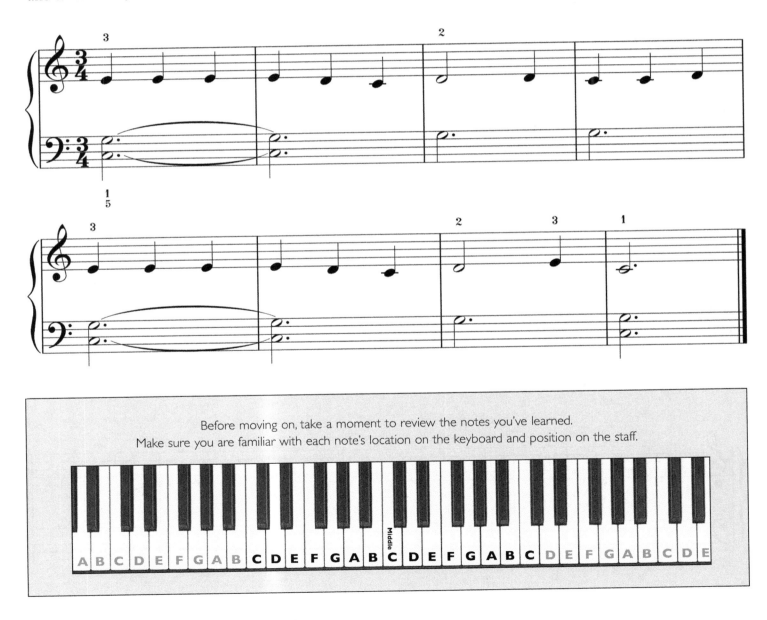

Before moving on, take a moment to review the notes you've learned.
Make sure you are familiar with each note's location on the keyboard and position on the staff.

Humoresque *Antonín Dvořák*

Here is another song in 3/4 time. Remember to place a slight emphasis on the first beat of each bar so that you really feel the waltz rhythm.

Listen to the demonstration on **Track 36** and then play along with the backing track on **Track 37**.

Chords

When you play more than one note simultaneously, this is called a **chord**. You can play a chord with the left hand or the right hand, or with both hands at the same time. There are many different types of chords, but here are a few that you can master in seconds.

C major

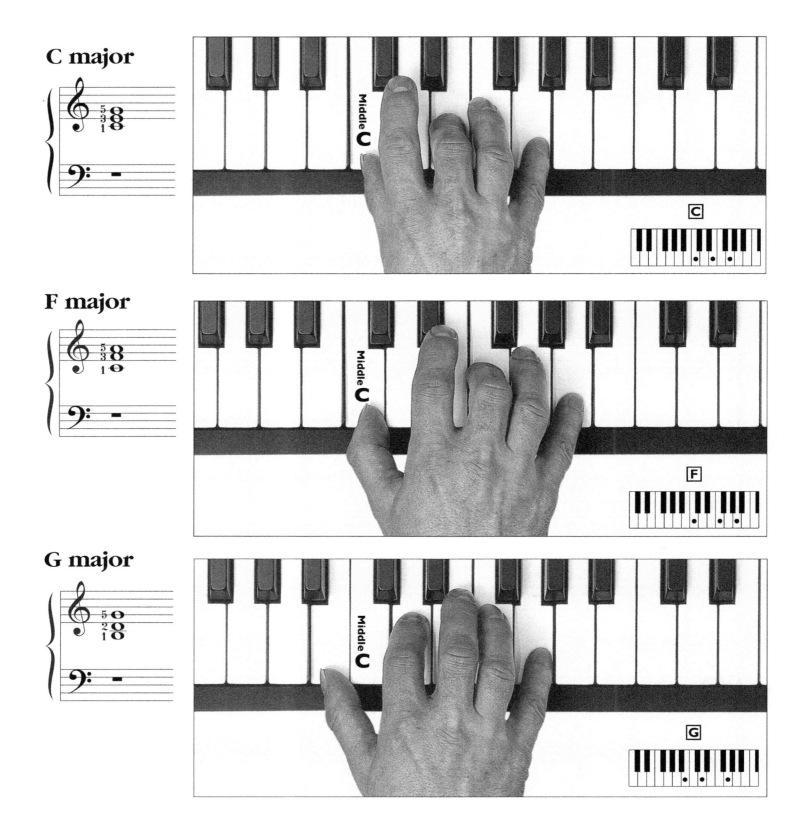

F major

G major

In this book, you'll be playing chords in which most of the notes are played by the right hand. Eventually you will be able to add more and more notes to these chords and involve the left hand as well.

The next piece of music features chords. Before you try this piece, look carefully at the fingerings, as they differ slightly from the standard chord fingerings you have just learned.

This is because when you are moving from one chord to another, you need to prepare the hand so that the transition from one chord to the next is smooth.

Take a look at the first two bars. To move smoothly to the second chord, which is played with fingers 1, 3, and 5, you need to prepare by playing the first chord with fingers 1, 2, and 4. When the first chord comes back again in bar 5 you can use the standard 1-3-5 fingering because this will help you get to the chord in bar 6, which is played with fingers 1, 2, and 5.

Concentrate on mastering these fingerings, as they will help you to play even the most complicated chord progressions with ease!

Listen to the demonstration on **Track 38** and then play along with the backing track on **Track 39**.

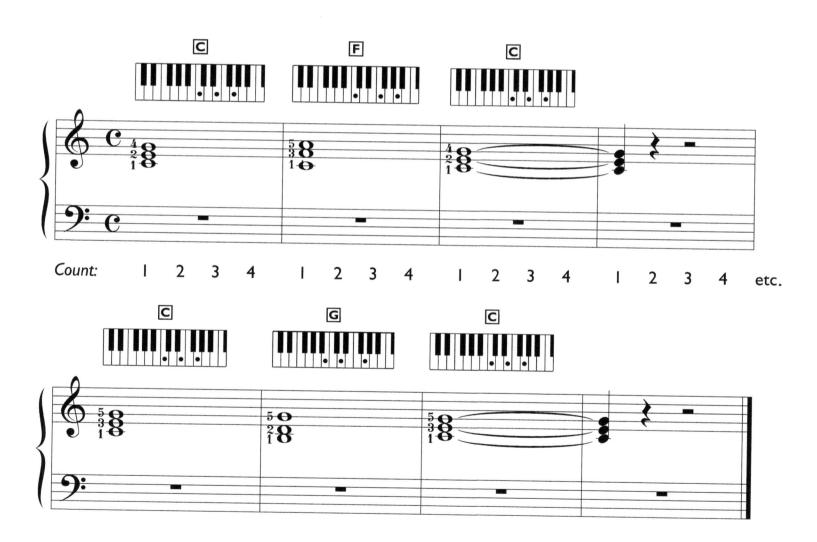

Chords with Both Hands

Now let's add the left hand. The left and right hands share the job of playing the notes that make up a chord. The left hand often plays fewer notes than the right hand, and they are more widely spaced.

Practice the exercise on the next page one hand at a time. You already know the right-hand part, as it's exactly the same as in the previous exercise, but now you will be adding single notes in the left hand.

Remember: when you are playing chords, hand and finger position are especially important. From the one basic hand position you have been using so far, you should be able to play this exercise without moving your hands away from the keys.

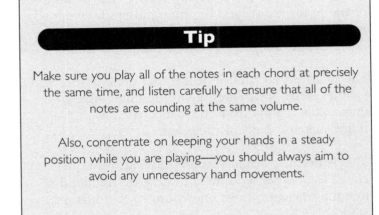

Tip

Make sure you play all of the notes in each chord at precisely the same time, and listen carefully to ensure that all of the notes are sounding at the same volume.

Also, concentrate on keeping your hands in a steady position while you are playing—you should always aim to avoid any unnecessary hand movements.

C major

F major

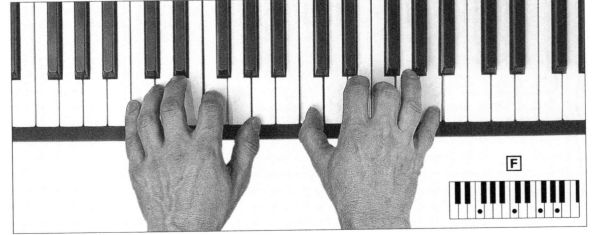

G major

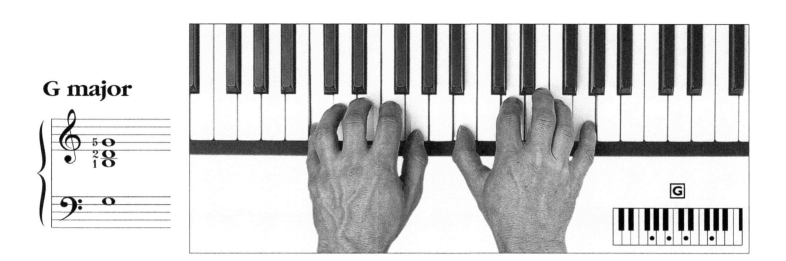

Now play the exercise below, and remember to watch your fingering—try to move as smoothly as possible from one chord to the next.

Listen to the demonstration on **Track 40** and then play along with the backing track on **Track 41**.

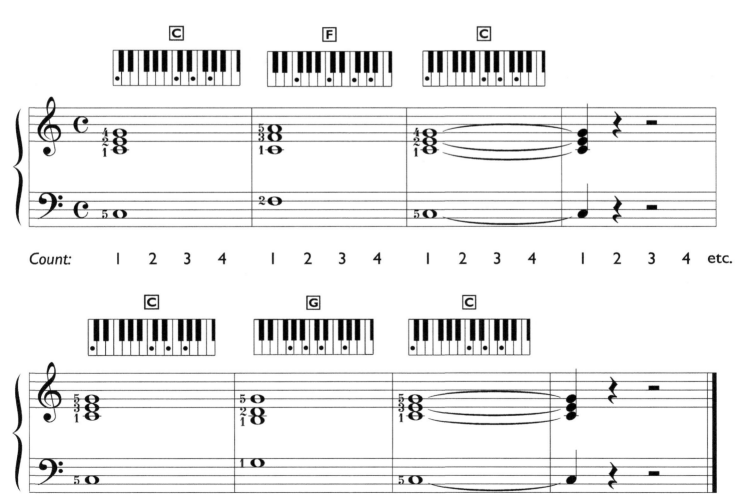

Count: 1 2 3 4 1 2 3 4 1 2 3 4 1 2 3 4 etc.

Moving the Right Hand

In this exercise, your right hand moves between G and A while the left hand remains steady.

Remember that the quarter notes in the right hand have a count of one beat each, while the whole notes in the left hand have a count of four beats each.

Watch out for the sudden stop at the end, where you only play on the first beat of the bar and then rest.

Listen to the demonstration on **Track 42** and then play along with the backing track on **Track 43**.

Here's an exercise for moving your left hand while keeping your right hand in place. The left hand is moving every two beats—be careful to keep the lower note (a C) constant while you move to the A with your thumb.

Also, notice that in the last bar you play for two beats and then rest for two beats.

Listen to the demonstration on **Track 44** and then play along with the backing track on **Track 45**.

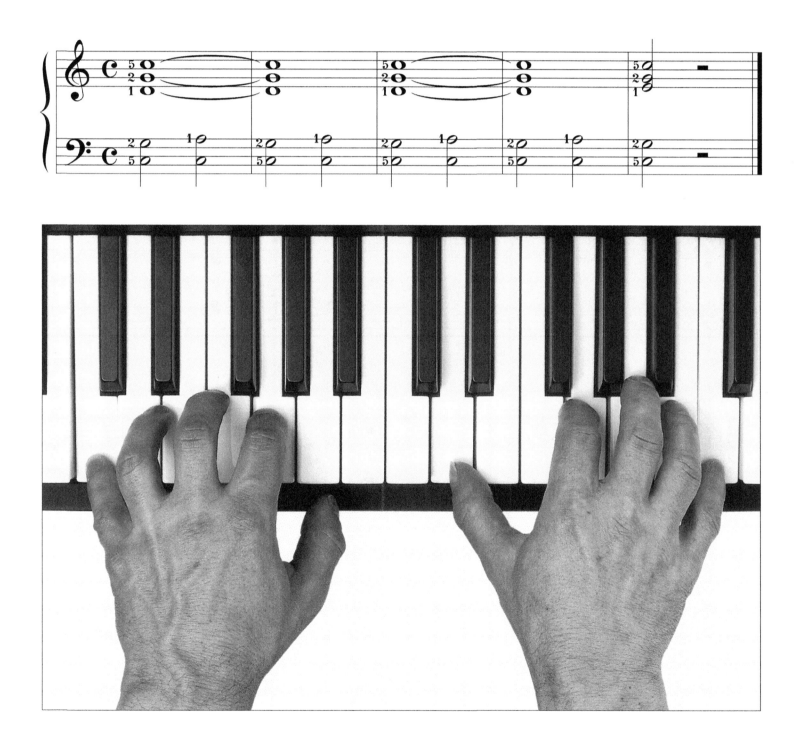

Oh, When The Saints *Traditional*

Here is a well-known song that will help you practice moving your left-hand chords. Play through it slowly at first until you are comfortable with the movement.

Be sure to keep the left hand steady, and don't forget to count!

Listen to the demonstration on **Track 46** and then play along with the backing track on **Track 47**.

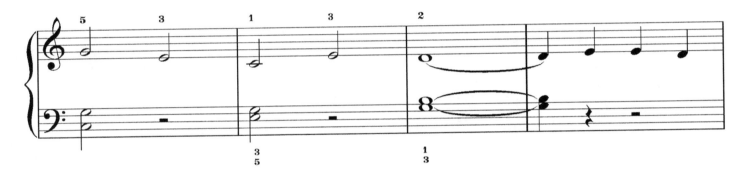

On Top Of Old Smoky *Traditional*

Now practice your left-hand chords with this popular tune! Follow the suggested fingerings carefully so that your hand stays in the correct position.

Listen to the demonstration on **Track 48** and then play along with the backing track on **Track 49**.

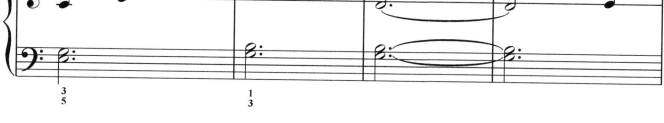

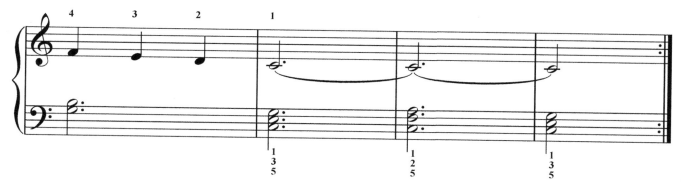

Ode to Joy *Ludwig van Beethoven*

Here is an extended version of Beethoven's "Ode To Joy" for both hands. There are some eighth-note patterns that you may find tricky at first.

Take a look at the right-hand notes in bar 8, where you play a dotted quarter note followed by an eighth note and then four eighth notes in a row. Practice this very slowly in each hand separately at first.

Also notice that, in bar 12, the melody switches from right to left hand. Follow the fingering suggested and make sure that you let go of the right-hand D before you play the left-hand G.

Listen to the demonstration on **Track 50** and then play along with the backing track on **Track 51**.

Largo from "New World" Symphony *Antonín Dvořák*

In this piece, you will see some new instructions: **Fine** and **D.C. al Fine** signs. This means that a section of the piece is to be repeated.

Listen to the demonstration on **Track 52** and then play along with the backing track on **Track 53**.

Once you have reached the end, the words "D.C. al Fine" tell you to start again at the beginning, and stop when you reach the word "Fine" meaning "end."

Fine

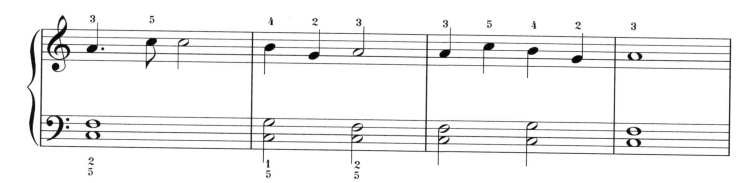

D.C. al Fine

Lullaby *Johannes Brahms*

Here is a piece of music that presents a new challenge. Although you know all of the notes, you will be moving away slightly from your usual hand position, so you'll need to pay close attention to your fingering. Notice that although you start on E, you begin with your thumb instead of finger 3.

Follow the suggested fingerings carefully so that your hand stays in the correct position.

Listen to the demonstration on **Track 54** and then play along with the backing track on **Track 55**.

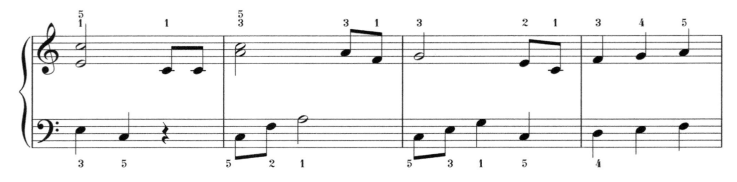

WELL DONE!

You now know the basics of playing the piano and reading music,
and are well on your way to becoming a proficient pianist.

Keep practicing the pieces and the concepts
you have learned in this book and soon you'll be able to
get around the piano keyboard with confidence.

Online Audio Track Listing

1. Your First Piece, demonstration
2. Your First Piece, backing track
3. C, D, and E, demonstration
4. C, D, and E, backing track
5. Merrily We Roll Along, demonstration
6. Merrily We Roll Along, backing track
7. Playing F to B, demonstration
8. Playing F to B, backing track
9. Lightly Row, demonstration
10. Lightly Row, backing track
11. Au Clair De La Lune, demonstration
12. Au Clair De La Lune, backing track
13. Ode To Joy, demonstration
14. Ode To Joy, backing track
15. Frère Jacques, demonstration
16. Frère Jacques, backing track
17. Notes and Rests, demonstration
18. Notes and Rests, backing track
19. Bass In Fourths, demonstration
20. Bass In Fourths, backing track
21. Ties and Rests, demonstration
22. Ties and Rests, backing track
23. Kum Ba Yah, demonstration
24. Kum Ba Yah, backing track
25. Little Brown Jug, demonstration
26. Little Brown Jug, backing track
27. Trumpet Voluntary, demonstration
28. Trumpet Voluntary, backing track
29. Eighth Notes, demonstration
30. Eighth Notes, backing track
31. Dotted Notes, demonstration
32. Dotted Note Exercise, demonstration
33. Dotted Note Exercise, backing track
34. Waltz Rhythm, demonstration
35. Waltz Rhythm, backing track
36. Humoresque, demonstration
37. Humoresque, backing track
38. Chords, demonstration
39. Chords, backing track
40. Chords with Both Hands, demonstration
41. Chords with Both Hands, backing track
42. Moving the Right Hand, demonstration
43. Moving the Right Hand, backing track
44. Moving the Left Hand, demonstration
45. Moving the Left Hand, backing track
46. Oh, When The Saints, demonstration
47. Oh, When The Saints, backing track
48. On Top Of Old Smoky, demonstration
49. On Top Of Old Smoky, backing track
50. Ode To Joy, demonstration
51. Ode To Joy, backing track
52. Largo, demonstration
53. Largo, backing track
54. Lullaby, demonstration
55. Lullaby, backing track